AXIS PARENT GUIDES SERIES

A Parent's Guide to the Sex Talk

A Parent's Guide to Pornography

A Parent's Guide to Sexual Assault

A Parent's Guide to Suicide & Self-Harm Prevention

A Parent's Guide to Depression & Anxiety

PARENT GUIDE BUNDLES

Parent Guides to Social Media

Parent Guides to Finding True Identity

Parent Guides to Mental & Sexual Health

A PARENT'S GUIDE TO
THE SEX TALK

A PARENT'S GUIDE TO

THE SEX TALK

Tyndale House Publishers
Carol Stream, Illinois

Visit Tyndale online at tyndale.com.

Visit Axis online at axis.org.

Tyndale and Tyndale's quill logo are registered trademarks of Tyndale House Ministries.

A Parent's Guide to the Sex Talk

For information about special discounts for bulk purchases, please contact Tyndale House Publishers at csresponse@tyndale.com, or call 1-855-277-9400.

Library of Congress Cataloging-in-Publication Data

A catalog record for this book is available from the Library of Congress.

ISBN 978-1-4964-6754-6

Printed in the United States of America

29	28	27	26	25	24	23
7	6	5	4	3	2	1

I want to be able to share God's great design
for sex.... I want God's voice to be stronger
than the voice of today's sexualized culture.

JEFF FISHER,
COVENANT EYES

Many families hope to protect their children
from radical ideas by walling off the secular
world—supervising what books they read,
what movies they see, what music they listen
to. But secular worldviews do not come
neatly labeled so we can easily recognize
them. Instead they mutate into forms that we
hardly recognize, becoming part of the very
air we breathe. The most powerful worldviews
are the ones we absorb without knowing it.
They are the ideas nobody talks about—the
assumptions we pick up almost by osmosis.

NANCY R. PEARCEY,
*LOVE THY BODY: ANSWERING HARD QUESTIONS
ABOUT LIFE AND SEXUALITY*

CONTENTS

A LETTER FROM AXIS

Dear Reader,

We're Axis, and since 2007, we've been creating resources to help connect parents, teens, and Jesus in a disconnected world. We're a group of gospel-minded researchers, speakers, and content creators, and we're excited to bring you the best of what we've learned about making meaningful connections with the teens in your life.

This parent's guide is designed to help start a conversation. Our goal is to give you enough knowledge that you're able to ask your teen informed questions about their world. For each guide, we spend weeks reading, researching, and interviewing parents and teens in order to distill everything you need to know about the topic at hand. We encourage you to read the whole thing and then to use the questions we include to get the conversation going with your teen—and then to follow the conversation wherever it leads.

As Douglas Stone, Bruce Patton, and Sheila Heen point out in their book *Difficult Conversations*, "Changes in attitudes and behavior rarely come about because of arguments, facts, and attempts to persuade. How often do *you* change your values and beliefs—or whom you love or what you want in life—based on something someone tells you? And how likely are you to do so when the person who is trying to change you doesn't seem fully aware of the reasons you see things differently in the first place?"[1] For whatever reason, when we believe that others are trying to understand *our* point of view, our defenses usually go down, and we're more willing to listen to *their* point of view. The rising generation is no exception.

So we encourage you to ask questions, to listen, and then to share your heart with your teen. As we often say at Axis, discipleship happens where conversation happens.

Sincerely,
Your friends at Axis

---

[1] Douglas Stone, Bruce Patton, and Sheila Heen, *Difficult Conversations: How to Discuss What Matters Most*, rev. ed. (New York: Penguin Books, 2010), 137.

FORGET HAVING JUST ONE "TALK" – WE NEED TO TALK TO OUR KIDS ABOUT SEX EARLY AND OFTEN

AT THE TIME OF DRAFTING THIS GUIDE, Snapchat was featuring a story called "Crazy Photos of Naked Couples in Vacuum Packs" while also offering a channel called "Cosmo after Dark" that, in its own words, "is an X-rated weekly edition that goes live every Friday at 6 p.m. and is exclusively dedicated to all things hot and h*rny." In addition, if you spend enough time on Instagram, you have a very good chance of encountering sexually explicit images, even if you are exploring topics unrelated to sex. We could point to countless other examples of the hypersexualization of our culture, from advertising to the average popular song or TV show. And that's without even mentioning the ease with which porn finds people online, whether they are looking for it or not.

We mention these examples in order to emphasize the fact that culture is having a never-ending conversation with our kids (and all of us really) about sex.[1] Because of the internet and the smartphone, culture is starting that conversation with our children earlier than ever. We parents can no longer afford to have only one sex talk with our kids or give them a book to read when they hit puberty. By then, it's too late. We must start the conversation about sex early, and we must continue that conversation as our children grow.

Because of the internet and the smartphone, culture is starting [the sex talk] with our children earlier than ever.... We must start the conversation about sex early, and we must continue that conversation as our children grow.

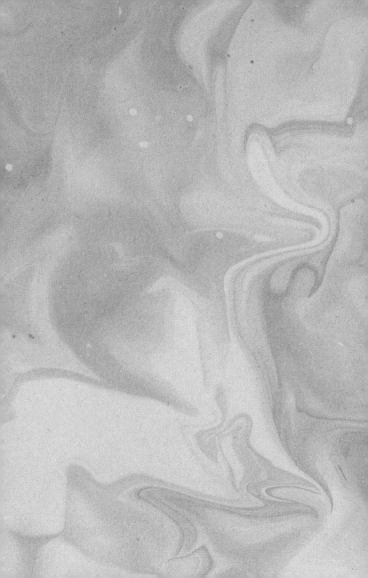

WHAT HAS THE SEX TALK LOOKED LIKE OVER THE YEARS?

MILLENNIALS (those born between the early 1980s and the mid-1990s)[2] probably experienced some version of "the talk," particularly if they grew up in Christian homes. This likely consisted of having one (probably awkward) conversation about sex or maybe going on a weekend trip where either Mom or Dad explained the ins and outs of puberty. While this strategy is inadequate in today's world, it is definitely a benefit that so many parents made an effort to have at least one conversation with their kids about sex. Having one talk is better than not having any.

Millennials' parents (typically baby boomers, born between roughly 1946 and 1964)[3] were even less likely to hear from their parents about sex. One baby boomer we talked to thinks she learned about it in a sex ed class at her school. Her own mother never explained sex to her.

Another baby boomer we talked to didn't hear from his parents about sex either. He ended up getting his information through a friend of his—and the friend had some pretty bizarre and inaccurate ideas. We talked to a Gen Xer (born between roughly the early 1960s and 1981)[4] who said his dad tried giving him the sex talk one week before his wedding, when he was 26! So it's good that later generations are starting to make an effort to educate their teens and preteens about sex before they've either had sex or learned a ton about it from culture.

Something interesting about the generations that preceded the baby boomers is that, while they tended never to talk about sex,[5] they also lived during a time when farming was more widespread. So it was more common for some of them to know about the mechanics of sex from being around farm animals, even if their parents never talked to them about it.[6]

But there is a reason why the sex talk is called "the talk." The very name implies that parents will only initiate one talk with their children when they start going through puberty, after which the parents will not need to bring up the topic again. After all, what teenagers want to talk with Mom or Dad about sex if they can possibly avoid it?

WHY DOES THE SEX TALK NEED TO CHANGE?

THE MAJORITY OF KIDS are exposed to porn by age thirteen, with some exposed as young as seven, according to a 2020 survey. It is more difficult today to find a man who has never encountered porn than to find one who has. Porn use has also become more common among females. Approximately 84 percent of males and 57 percent of females are exposed before they turn eighteen.[7] Many are identifying the average age of first exposure to porn as eleven years old. Keep in mind that, because this is an average, there are children even younger than that who are seeing porn. In fact, 10 percent of children who encounter porn online are under the age of ten.[8]

Among the reviews for the book *Good Pictures Bad Pictures: Porn-Proofing Today's Young Kids*, one user commented, "I personally sought out this book for my

6-year-old when he tearfully reported seeing naked people on a 6-year-old friend's phone. My son was not able to verbalize what he had seen."[9] The threat of pornography is enough of a reason in itself for parents to start the conversation about sex long before their children reach puberty. For comprehensive info and advice on the dangers of porn, see our *A Parent's Guide to Pornography* booklet.

Another reason why "the talk" needs to change is one we have already mentioned: culture is sending out a constant barrage of confusing and conflicting messages about gender and sexuality. If you do not preempt the conversation about sex with your children, then culture, the internet, and their friends *will* shape their beliefs about sexuality.

If you do not preempt the conversation about sex with your children, then culture, the internet, and their friends will shape their beliefs about sexuality.

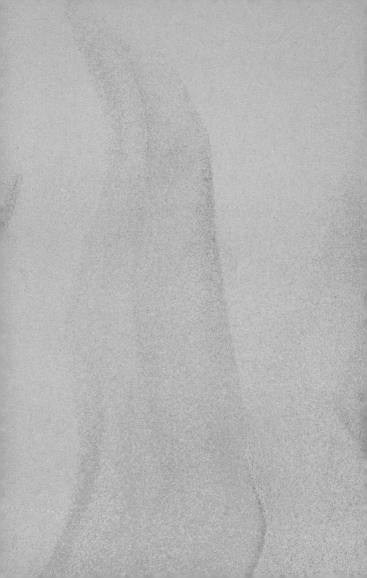

WHAT STOPS PARENTS FROM TALKING TO THEIR KIDS ABOUT SEX?

COVENANT EYES points out several reasons why parents avoid talking to their kids about sex.[10] One is that the parents themselves don't have good examples of how to have these conversations. It's more common for people to have had a bad experience with the sex talk than to have had a good one, and it's much easier to do something well when we've seen it modeled well for us. So it's understandable that many parents are at a loss regarding how to talk with their kids about sex. Nevertheless, it's crucial that we figure out how to do this well.[11]

Possibly the most obvious reason for avoiding these conversations is that talking to our kids about sex is uncomfortable. Many parents are extremely concerned about their kids' sexual decisions but won't bring up the topic. Yes, it's awkward, but our kids need us to move past any reluctance we have and face the challenge head-on. *The more we talk to our kids about sex, especially if we start when they're young, the less awkward it will be.* Believe it or not, our kids *do* want to hear from us about sex and relationships.

Note that *moms and dads both need to be on board.* In an interview with Axis, Craig Gross, founder of XXXchurch (xxxchurch. com), says that the majority of questions he sees from parents about how to talk to their kids about sex come from women, and not just women who are single mothers. Even when dads are present in their families and have sons, they are often passive instead of engaged. Sons need their fathers to take the lead in discipling their sexuality. But moms aren't always proactive about it, either. American life tends to be quite busy, and many parents are not having key conversations with their kids because they're just

The more we talk to our kids about sex, especially if we start when they're young, the less awkward it will be. Believe it or not, our kids do want to hear from us about sex and relationships.

trying to keep their heads above water and get everyone where they need to go without being *too* late (can we get an *amen?*). Again, this is understandable, but it's critical that we don't let ourselves be distracted from having these discussions.

Many people find out about sex from some source other than their parents. It can be easy for parents to make the excuse that their kids will turn out fine, even if they don't hear about sex in the ideal way. That may be true, but it's a dangerous gamble, particularly since technology has made porn so accessible to young children. (Even if our kids don't have devices or have strict restrictions on them, it's not possible to make sure all their friends are under similar restrictions.) If we take this gamble, we're surrendering our responsibilities and choosing to let culture shape our children's sexuality.

Some of us might feel that our past sexual failures disqualify us as credible authorities. But this just isn't true. Our kids can learn valuable lessons from both our successes and our failures if we are willing to be vulnerable with them and share how God has worked in our life. Consider sharing how you wish you could change your past based on what you know now, or how your choices brought about harm instead of good.

On the other hand, if we have unhealthy views about sex or are currently caught up in sexual sin, we will not be able to be the mentors our kids need us to be. If we are addicted to porn or masturbation or are being unfaithful to our spouse, we are not equipped to teach our kids how to honor God in the area of sexuality. We must seek healing for ourselves first.

WHAT PRINCIPLES SHOULD I FOLLOW WHEN I'M TALKING TO MY KIDS ABOUT SEX?

EVERY FAMILY AND EVERY PERSON IS UNIQUE. How you talk to your kids about sex will depend on what works best for your family and the personalities of your individual children. So we're not going to tell you exactly how you should have these discussions with your kids because doing so requires wisdom and discernment. But there are principles you can follow and creatively apply in your home.

1. TEACH YOUR KIDS HOW TO ENGAGE WELL WITH CULTURE.

A couple we talked to makes sure they do not avoid their kids' questions about *anything*. They don't want the internet, culture, or their kids' friends to be the ones answering their children's questions. They teach their kids how to critically think about and interact with life situations instead of choosing the more natural (and culturally encouraged) inclinations to follow their feelings, mindlessly believe what others tell them—or hide from secular culture out of fear. They also have discussions with each other about their own beliefs in front of their kids. This way, their kids observe how their parents process ideas and learn how to analyze culture from watching that example.

2. MAKE SURE YOUR KIDS KNOW THAT NO TOPIC IS OFF-LIMITS.

According to Craig Gross, "Your kids will talk to you about things you talk to them about. Your kids won't talk to you about things you don't talk to them about." It's not necessary to go into explicit detail about sexual topics with younger children, but don't be afraid to give them an honest answer. One dad we spoke with says, "I'd rather my kids be comfortable having a weird conversation with me than go somewhere else to find their answers."

One of the daughters of the couple mentioned previously asked what adultery was. When answering her, the dad used an analogy that she could understand, comparing adultery to betrayal. He didn't go into graphic detail and didn't even mention that adultery had anything to do with sex. But he also didn't avoid her question or imply that the topic was forbidden. Notably, she asked this question because the family was working through the Ten Commandments during their Bible study time. Often, these conversations can be organic and natural if your kids know you are a safe place to go to when questions arise.

3. BE DIRECT.

When your kids feel comfortable coming to you and asking you a question about sex, answer them directly. If you are evasive, they might conclude that you and/or Christianity do not have good answers or that the answers are inadequate. They could infer that sex is embarrassing and shameful. These would be false and destructive conclusions. You might feel uncomfortable, but would you rather your kids discover what, say, an orgasm is from you? Or would you rather they turned to their friends or the Internet?

As your kids are learning their body parts, use the actual names for those parts and avoid unnecessary euphemisms when you're explaining sex to them. There's nothing shameful about saying "vagina" or "penis." They need to know these terms, and being straightforward with them in the beginning will save them from confusion later. Using made-up words only leaves room for misunderstanding and implies that our sexuality is taboo instead of a normal and good part of how God created us. There is a real

How you talk to your kids about sex will depend on what works best for your family and the personalities of your individual children.

danger to the long-term sexual health of your children if you portray sex as dirty, wrong, or mysterious. They must learn that it is good, created by God, and made to function properly within the confines of marriage.

4. MAKE SURE YOU AND YOUR SPOUSE ARE ON THE SAME PAGE.

You're much less likely to talk to your kids about something that you don't talk to your spouse about. If you can't talk about sex with your spouse, then you won't be able to talk about it with your kids. Even if you don't have issues to resolve with your spouse, it's important that you both have a unified game plan to educate your kids about sex.

5. BE PROACTIVE. (START EARLY.)

If you wait till your kids ask you questions about sex, *it will be too late*. You need to be proactive in raising the subject, keeping in mind that, sadly, it could even be too late if you wait till your kids start elementary school. If you want to be the one to shape your kids' views about sex, you must start early. How early you begin is up to you, but we don't think it's too extreme to say parents should be explaining some facts about sex to their kids as soon as the kids are able to talk. Again, we're not saying you should go into graphic detail or inundate them with everything they'll eventually need to know. We are saying that you should *have age-appropriate conversations early*.

There are several advantages to starting the conversation about sex when your kids are young. First, it's much easier to talk about sex when your relationships with your kids are not in crisis (for

It is vital that you create a
family culture where your
kids know they can talk to
you about anything.

example, if you've caught them viewing porn). Second, younger children are naturally curious and open. They have not yet hit the awkward stage or become reticent teenagers. Parents of elementary-age children have a great opportunity to encourage their kids to come to them with questions, making it much likelier that their kids will still be willing to do so when they reach adolescence.

One couple we spoke with has been using the book series God's Design for Sex to talk to their children at different age levels. The parents haven't gotten to the books for older kids yet because their kids aren't teenagers, but they have found the first two books very helpful. A structured series like this is a great option, especially if you feel at a loss regarding how to initiate these conversations.

6. DON'T RELY ON SCARE TACTICS.

Don't rely on the threat of STIs or pregnancy as the reasons why your kids should avoid sex. In the heat of the moment, few teens will find these arguments compelling. It is valid to communicate that having sex outside of marriage could lead to diseases or pregnancy, but be careful how you communicate those consequences. Mentioning disease and pregnancy at the same time implies that pregnancy is like a disease. This argument also focuses on negative reasons for not having sex outside of marriage instead of positive reasons for having it within marriage. It says nothing about the fact that both sex and children are blessings from God.

7. EMPHASIZE THAT SEX IS GOOD AND BEAUTIFUL AND THAT IT IS GOD'S IDEA.

Make sure your kids know that God created sex and that He created it very good.

There is a real danger to the long-term sexual health of your children if you portray sex as dirty, wrong, or mysterious. They must learn that it is good, created by God, and made to function properly within the confines of marriage.

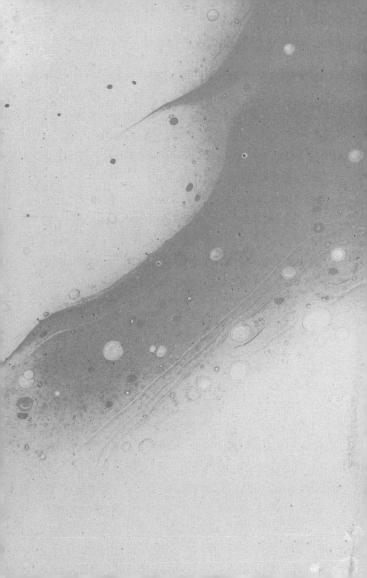

Sex has multiple purposes, but one of them is to give pleasure. It's easy to forget about the Song of Songs, but there's a reason the Scriptures include a book that unabashedly celebrates romantic, sexual love! When God gave us the gift of sex, He also gave us the beautiful and sobering ability to create life. Because God is our Creator and the Creator of our sexuality, *He* is the one who gets to say what sex is and how we should use it. *He is good, so His plan for sex is what will lead to our flourishing.*

As your kids get older, explain to them that sex is part of an earthly picture of a cosmic reality. The Bible makes it clear that marriage between one man and one woman symbolizes Christ's relationship with the church. Quoting Genesis 2:24, Paul writes in Ephesians 5:31-32, "'For this reason a man will leave his father and mother and be united to his wife, and the two will become one flesh.' This is a profound mystery—but I am talking about Christ and the church."

Marriage is in many ways a metaphor for the Trinity lived out in the flesh. So if people abuse God's design for sexuality, they are living out a lie about God Himself. This is arguably one of the best reasons we have for being careful to obey God in this area of our lives.

8. BE CREATIVELY DISCERNING AND KEEP THE CONVERSATION GOING.

There are many options for raising the topic of sex with your kids. You could use the God's Design for Sex series we mentioned, or you could use the Bible. Using the Bible for these discussions is helpful because you'll want to explain God's purpose for sex at some point

Whether or not you overtly make the Bible part of your strategy, you should certainly be prepared to answer any questions your kids have about sex when they read about it in the Bible.

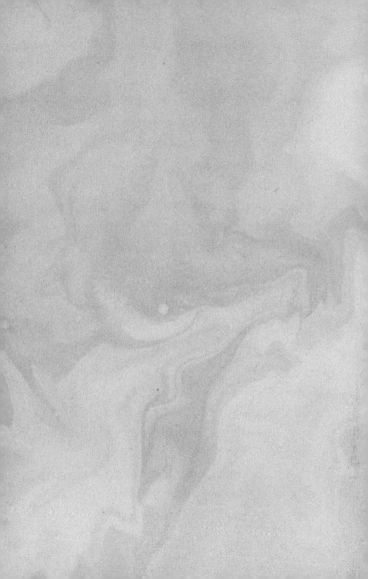

anyway. Whether or not you overtly make the Bible part of your strategy, you should certainly be prepared to answer any questions your kids have about sex when they read about it in the Bible. The great thing about the Bible is that it portrays both healthy and unhealthy views of sexuality, as well as the consequences of both. The myriad of stories from David and Bathsheba to Samson and Delilah to Joseph and Potiphar's wife could prompt incredible conversations about the life-long impacts of good and bad choices pertaining to sex.

One man we spoke to says that when he was about ten years old, his dad took him and his older brother on a weekend trip. The dad didn't bill the trip as a rite of manhood or as time to talk about sex and puberty. He kept the entire outing very low-key, just the three of them having an adventure. In the car, however, they listened to the audiobook of Dr. James Dobson's *Preparing for Adolescence*. The man remembers that listening to the book was awkward, but what really stands out in his memory is how fun and adventurous the trip was and the fact that his dad and brother weren't afraid to talk about awkward topics with him. The tone of the trip and sense of community his dad fostered were possibly even more important than the content of the audiobook. It was also very helpful that his dad didn't make the weekend into a big deal but kept it laid-back and low-pressure.

However you decide to broach the topic of sex with your kids, you should use their experiences and everyday situations to keep their sexual education ongoing. You could use stories you read to them, shows they watch, their school experiences, or anything else that comes to mind. Be creative and discerning.

One dad we know told us the story of a time when he and his son were driving somewhere, and his son saw a billboard with a crude advertisement for a medical checkup. His son laughed at it, but it turned out he didn't really understand what the ad was talking about. So the dad used that opportunity as a teaching moment. There is no one right way to go about having these conversations. *Just remember to be proactive, not passive.*

9. KEEP A FEW OTHER THINGS IN MIND.

Hopefully you will start these conversations early, but make sure you tell your kids about puberty *before* their bodies start changing. Prepare them for what is going to happen to them.[12] It's scary and unnerving, especially for girls, to go through puberty with no idea what's going on! If you don't help them through that experience, they'll probably turn to their friends or to the internet. In that case, they will have a good chance of getting erroneous information at best or hurtful information at worst. We talked to one woman who was at a doctor's appointment when she first learned about menstrual cycles because the doctor asked her mother if she had started hers yet. Luckily, her mom used the opportunity to explain it to her daughter in the car on the way home from the appointment. The daughter began her cycle for the first time only a few months later! She was eleven years old.

Even though your goal is to have these conversations often so they're not as awkward as they could be, when you're planning to talk to your kids about sex it's

Even though your goal is to have these conversations often so they're not as awkward as they could be, when you're planning to talk to your kids about sex it's still wise to take your environment into account.

still wise to take your environment into account. If you expect to be uncomfortable, maybe go on a walk so you're moving instead of staring at each other across a table.

For the most part, talking to your kids about sex will be most comfortable and beneficial if mothers talk with daughters and fathers talk with sons. But it's also good at different times for both parents to speak into their child's life about sexual issues because then the child gets the perspective and wisdom of the opposite-sex parent.

An article from *Today's Parent* titled "How to Talk to Your Kids about Sex: An Age-by-Age Guide" provides some helpful advice on the conversations you should be having with your kids at different ages, as well as what sort of curiosity you should expect from them at different ages.[13] For example, it's normal for toddlers to explore their body parts, whether in private or public. Instead of shaming them for this, straightforwardly explain the proper behavior of people in public, and don't make a big deal about what they're doing.

Don't forget that one of your goals in educating your kids about sex is to protect them from sexual predators. Make it very clear that certain types of touch are inappropriate and that they should tell you immediately if anyone wants to touch them in a wrong way. We recommend that you apply this same idea to technology, even if you are not letting your kids use devices yet. Remember, they could see something explicit on one of their friends' devices. Let your kids know that if they see images online that show naked people or that scare them, they need to tell you right away and you won't be angry. Encourage them that, far from being upset, you'll be incredibly thankful that they trusted you enough to tell you about what they saw.

When your kids become teenagers, it might be easy for you to think that they're not interested in hearing from you. It's important that you continue to disciple them about sex, no matter how awkward it feels and no matter how reluctant they seem. There are a myriad of issues related to sexuality (such as dating, porn, sexting, and so on) about which they will need guidance from you.

DISCUSSION QUESTIONS

BELOW ARE SOME SUGGESTED QUESTIONS you might raise with your kids. *Remember, these are guidelines!* Precisely when and how you ask these questions is up to you. Note: There are not many questions in the Middle School and Older section. This might seem odd since, at those ages, kids are exposed to so much talk of sexuality, thanks to our culture. While you should absolutely have many ongoing conversations about sex with your kids, this guide focuses on *introducing* the topic of sex and encouraging your kids to be comfortable talking to you about it. The majority of questions below are for preschool and elementary ages because we believe those are the key times you should be educating your kids about what sex is.

PRESCHOOL

1. Do you know what all your body parts are called?

2. Do you know how boys are different from girls?

3. Do you know which places no one should be touching you?

4. Do you know that if anyone touches you in a way that you don't like, you can say no?[14]

5. Do you know what to do if someone touches you somewhere they shouldn't?

6. Do you know that you can talk to us about anything?

7. Do you know where babies come from? (We're putting this question here because it is possible kids could ask it this early.)[15]

ELEMENTARY SCHOOL

1. Do you feel comfortable coming to us with any questions you have about sex? If not, how can we help?

2. Can you tell me what you already know about _____?

3. What have you heard about _____?

4. Do you know what sex is?

5. Do you know what puberty is?

6. Do you know what will happen when you go through puberty? Do you understand how your body is going to change?

7. Do you know about other changes that could happen during puberty (mood swings, acne, etc.)?

8. Do you know what God tells us about sex (i.e., it's beautiful, it's meant to happen within marriage between one man and one woman, it's a way for a husband and wife to show they love each other)?

9. Do you understand that sex is powerful (i.e., it bonds us emotionally and physically, it comes with the ability to create life, etc.) and a great responsibility?

10. Do you know what masturbation is? Have you ever masturbated before?

11. Do you understand that it's normal and good to have sexual desires and feelings?

12. Do you know how to deal with those feelings when you have them?

How does understanding God's purpose for sex change how we think about it?

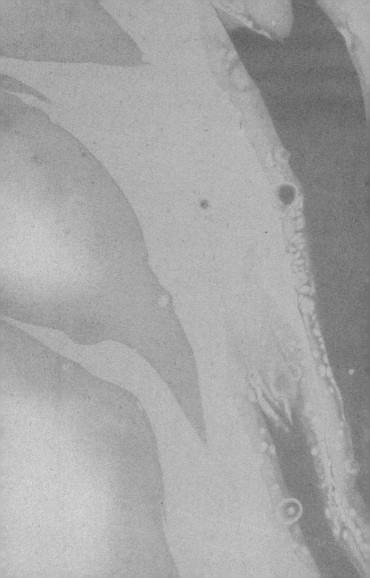

13. Do you know what to do if you see pictures of naked people?

14. Do you know what to do if you see something online that you don't understand or that scares you?

15. What do you think about _____?

FOR GIRLS:

16. Do you know what a period is? Do you know why girls have periods and what to expect when you start having yours?

17. Do you know if any of the other girls at school have started their periods yet?

FOR BOYS:

18. Do you know what erections are and why you have them?

19. Do you know what a wet dream is?

MIDDLE SCHOOL AND OLDER

1. How does understanding God's purpose for sex change how we think about it?

2. How have you seen your friends interact with the opposite sex in ways that seem positive? What about negative?

3. Do you think most of your peers treat each other with respect when it comes to flirting/sex/relationships? Explain.

4. How do your friends who aren't Christians think and talk about sex? How about your friends who are Christians?

5. What do you think about the romantic relationships in this movie/TV show?

6. What do you think about how women were portrayed in that show? What about how men were portrayed?

7. What do you think are the underlying assumptions of that commercial?

FINAL THOUGHTS

YOU HAVE NOTHING TO LOSE by being direct and honest with your kids about sex, especially if you keep the conversation going long-term and create a culture of openness. *Your kids need the wisdom you have.* If you are willing to be proactive about how you approach the sex *talks* with your kids, you have the phenomenal opportunity to position yourself as the one who shapes their understanding of sexuality to be God-honoring and fulfilling.

You have nothing to lose by being direct and honest with your kids about sex, especially if you keep the conversation going long-term and create a culture of openness.

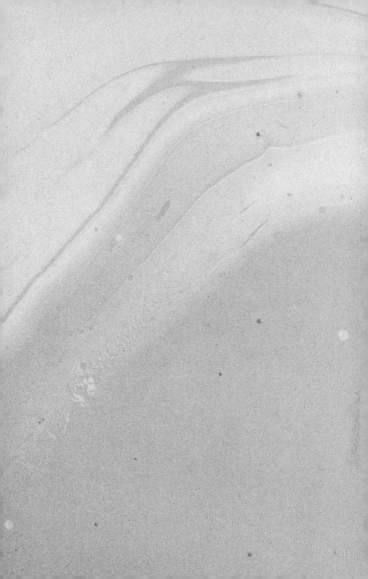

RECAP

- Because of the internet and the smartphone, culture is starting the conversation of sex with our children earlier than ever.

- "The talk" implies that parents will only have one talk with their children about sex when their kids start going through puberty, after which the parents will not bring up the topic again.

- Many identify the average age of first exposure to porn as eleven years old. The threat of pornography is enough of a reason for parents to start the conversation about sex long before their children reach puberty.

- Our culture sends out a constant barrage of confusing and conflicting messages about gender and sexuality. If we do not preempt the conversation about sex, then culture, the internet, and friends *will* shape our kids' beliefs about sexuality.

- *The more we talk to our kids about sex, especially if we start when they're young, the less awkward it will be.* Believe it or not, our kids *do* want to hear from us about sex and relationships.

- Moms and dads both need to be on board with these conversations.

- Some of us might feel that our past sexual failures disqualify us as credible authorities. But this just isn't true.

- It's key that we teach our kids how to engage well with culture.

- It is also vital to create a family culture where our kids know they can talk to us about anything.

- When our kids feel comfortable asking a direct question about sex, we should answer them directly.

- If we wait till our kids ask questions about sex, *it will be too late*. Have age-appropriate conversations early.

- Emphasize that sex is good and beautiful and that it is God's idea.

ADDITIONAL RESOURCES

Note: Axis does not necessarily agree with everything in all the resources we've listed below, and we disagree outright with some of the information they contain. But we have listed these resources because we believe they have some valuable content in them.

1. *Authentic Intimacy* blog, https://www.authenticintimacy.com/blog

2. *Java with Juli®* podcast, https://www.authenticintimacy.com/podcast

3. Juli Slattery, "Parenting as a Team," Authentic Intimacy, https://www.authenticintimacy.com/resources/8504/parenting-as-a-team

4. "Talking about Sex and Puberty with Your Kids," Focus on the Family, https://www.focusonthefamily.com/parenting/talking-about-sex-and-puberty/

5. Mary VanClay, "How to Talk to Your Child about Sex (Ages 6 to 8)," https://www.babycenter.com/child/parenting-strategies/how-to-talk-to-your-child-about-sex-ages-6-to-8_67908

6. XXXChurch, "Help for Parents," https:// xxxchurch.com/get-help/porn-addiction -help-for-parents

7. Craig Gross and David Dean, *Touchy Subjects: Talking to Kids about Sex, Tech, and Social Media in the Touchscreen World*

8. Ron DeHaas, "Talking to Your Kids about Sex: A Parent-Child Bible Study," Covenant Eyes, https://www.covenanteyes.com /2014/04/14/talking-about-sex-bible-study/

9. Sam Black, "Rethinking the Sex Talk (Part 1)," Covenant Eyes, https://www .covenanteyes.com/2012/06/26/rethinking -the-sex-talk-part-1/

10. Sam Black, "Rethinking the Sex Talk (Part 2)," Covenant Eyes, https://www .covenanteyes.com/2012/07/19/rethinking -the-sex-talk-part-2/

11. Traci Lester, *Teaching the Birds and the Bees without the Butterflies*

12. John A. Younts and David Younts, *Everyday Talk about Sex and Marriage: A Biblical Handbook for Parents*

13. Kristen A. Jenson and Gail Poyner, *Good Pictures Bad Pictures: Porn-Proofing Today's Young Kids*

14. Kristen A. Jenson, *Good Pictures Bad Pictures Jr.: A Simple Plan to Protect Young Minds*

15. Defend Young Minds Resources, https://www.defendyoungminds.com/products

16. Kristen A. Jenson, "The Sex Talk: Your Chance to Make a First Impression," Defend Young Minds, https://www.defendyoungminds.com/post/the-sex-talk-your-chance-to-make-a-first-impression

17. Kristen A. Jenson, "Mom's Dilemma: 'How Do I Teach Healthy Sexual Attitudes When I Don't Enjoy Sex?'" Defend Young Minds, https://www.defendyoungminds.com/post/moms-dilemma-teach-healthy-sexual-attitudes-dont-enjoy-sex

18. Marilyn Evans, "7 Things Your Seven-Year-Old Should Know about Love and Sex," Defend Young Minds, https://www.defendyoungminds.com/post/7-things-seven-year-old-should-know-love-sex

19. Kristen A. Jenson, "Will I Rob My Child's Innocence If I Start Talking about the Dangers of Porn?" Defend Young Minds, https://www.defendyoungminds.com/post/will-i-rob-childs-innocence

20. Marilyn Evans, "How to Talk to Kids about Porn: Research Reveals 5 Obstacles to Overcome," Defend Young Minds, https://www.defendyoungminds.com/post/how-to-talk-to-kids-about-porn

21. Kristen A. Jenson, "Warning Signs of Sexual Abuse—How to Protect Your Child," Defend Young Minds, https://www.defendyoungminds.com/post/warning-signs-child-sexual-abuse

22. Sheryl Lynn, "How to Talk to Kids about Sexuality: It's Not Just about Sex, Christian Author Says," *Christian Post*, https://www.christianpost.com/news/how-to-talk-to-kids-about-sexuality-its-not-just-about-sex-christian-author-says-186529/

23. "Talking to Kids about Sex," Parenting, https://www.parenting.com/child/talking-to-kids-about-sex-21335549/

NOTES

1. Angus Whyte, "How to Talk to an Internet-Obsessed Teen about Sex," Evolve Treatment Centers, accessed September 15, 2022, https://evolvetreatment.com/blog/talk -internet-obsessed-teen-sex/.

2. Michael Dimock, "Defining Generations: Where Millennials End and Generation Z Begins," Pew Research Center, January 17, 2019, https://www.pewresearch.org/fact -tank/2019/01/17/where-millennials-end-and -generation-z-begins/.

3. Philip Bump, "Here Is When Each Generation Begins and Ends, according to Facts," *Atlantic*, March 25, 2014, https://www.theatlantic.com /national/archive/2014/03/here-is-when-each -generation-begins-and-ends-according-to -facts/359589/.

4. "Generation X," Wikipedia, accessed September 15, 2022, https://en.wikipedia.org/wiki /Generation_X.

5. Nancy Casas, Emily Summerhayes, and Amber Hubert, "Talking Sex with Grandma,"

PrimeMind, May 4, 2016, https://primemind
.com/talking-sex-with-grandma-f8efcb12dedf
?gi=a2d92f08d042.

6. "How Much Did Our Grandparents Know
about Sex When They Were Teenagers?"
Quora, accessed September 15, 2022, https://
www.quora.com/How-much-did-our
-grandparents-know-about-sex-when-they
-were-teenagers.

7. "What's the Average Age of a Child's First
Exposure to Porn?" Fight the New Drug, April
21, 2022, https://fightthenewdrug.org/real
-average-age-of-first-exposure/.

8. "The Detrimental Effects of Pornography on
Small Children," Net Nanny, December 19,
2017, https://www.netnanny.com/blog/the
-detrimental-effects-of-pornography-on
-small-children/.

9. Kristen A. Jenson and Gail Poyner, *Good
Pictures Bad Pictures: Porn-Proofing Today's
Young Kids* (Kennewick, WA: Glen Cove Press,
2014), https://www.amazon.com/Good
-Pictures-Bad-Porn-Proofing-Todays/dp
/0615927335/ref=sr_1_1.

10. Cory M. Schortzman, "10 Reasons Parents Don't Talk to Children about Sex and Porn," Covenant Eyes, October 27, 2020, https://www.covenanteyes.com/2015/07/25/10-reasons-parents-dont-talk-to-children-about-sex-and-porn/.

11. Juli Slattery, "Sexual Discipleship®: What Is It, and Why Is It Important?" Authentic Intimacy, April 28, 2021, https://www.authenticintimacy.com/resources/2641/the-importance-of-sexual-discipleship and Phyllis Fagell, "How to Talk to Kids about Sex," *Washington Post*, August 30, 2017, https://www.washingtonpost.com/lifestyle/on-parenting/how-to-talk-to-kids-about-sex/2017/08/29/2c994fce-77c5-11e7-8839-ec48ec4cae25_story.html.

12. Rachel Pomerance Berl, "Teaching Your Kids about Sex: Do's and Don'ts," *U.S. News & World Report*, August 3, 2012, https://health.usnews.com/health-news/articles/2012/08/03/teaching-your-kids-about-sex-dos-and-donts.

13. Lindsay Kneteman, "How to Talk to Your Kids about Sex: An Age-by-Age Guide," *Today's Parent*, September 24, 2021, https://www

.todaysparent.com/family/parenting/age-by
-age-guide-to-talking-to-kids-about-sex/.

14. Erin Dower, "An Age-by-Age Guide to
    Teaching Kids about 'The Birds & the Bees,'"
    FamilyEducation, accessed September 17,
    2022, https://www.familyeducation.com/life
    /talking-about-sex/age-age-guide-teaching
    -kids-about-birds-bees.

15. "Talking to Your Kids about Sex," Familydoctor
    .org, May 14, 2020, https://familydoctor.org
    /talking-kids-sex/.

PARENT GUIDES TO SOCIAL MEDIA
BY AXIS

It's common to feel lost in your teen's world. Let these be your go-to guides on social media, how it affects your teen, and how to begin an ongoing conversation about faith that matters.

BUNDLE THESE 5 BOOKS AND SAVE

PARENT GUIDES TO FINDING TRUE IDENTITY
BY AXIS

When culture is constantly pulling teens away from Christian values, let these five parent guides spark an ongoing conversation about finding your true identity in Christ.

BUNDLE THESE 5 BOOKS AND SAVE

PARENT GUIDES TO MENTAL & SEXUAL HEALTH
BY AXIS

Don't let mainstream media be the only voice in your teens' conversations about mental and sexual health. Gain confidence and unravel your fears about breaching these sensitive topics today.

BUNDLE THESE 5 BOOKS AND SAVE

DISCOVER MORE PARENT GUIDES, VIDEOS, AND AUDIOS AT AXIS.ORG

axis
www.axis.org

CP1846